SAVVY SAYIN'S

by
KEN ALSTAD

An Old West Almanac publication

published by
Ken Alstad Company
Tucson, Arizona

First Printing: July, 1986
Second Printing: May, 1987
Third Printing: November, 1987
Fourth Printing: September, 1988
Fifth Printing: August, 1989
Sixth Printing: March, 1990
Seventh Printing: October, 1990
Eighth Printing: June, 1991
Ninth Printing: February, 1992

The illustrations in this book are from
the author's private collection.

The Savvy Sayin's in this book were published previously
in various copyrighted editions
of the Old West Almanac from 1980 to 1987.

The quotations appearing on the back cover and in the
introduction are from three general sources:
newspaper feature articles or book reviews on the
Old West Almanac, letters to the publisher, and
book reviews on earlier printings of "Savvy Sayin's"

ISBN: 0-96169-850-0

Printed in the United States of America.

Published by:
Ken Alstad Company
9096 East Bellevue Street
Tucson, Arizona 85715
602/298-0175

SAVVY
SAYIN'S

**The West is where Nature is apt to be
a mite exaggerated.**

*Illustration, following page: "A Halt in the
Yosemite Valley," by A. Bierstadt*

The future
has been losing
the wisdom of the past
ever since the freeway
bypassed the corral

Damn!

The American language and patterns of speech won't shut up and stand still. People keep stirring them — expecially the young when juices are boiling their blood.

Over the years some changes they made were as giddy as twenty-three-skidoo. Some took the joy out of words like gay. Some were linguistically lazy — like, you know, man, totally like dumb, you know. *But not all!*

Some have been smart, philosophical, or witty. But if they were caught in a corner of time, they became quaint, rustic, and forgotten. The future lost the wisdom of the past. *Damn!*

In Colonial America, Benjamin Franklin was the best-known author of one-liner wit and wisdom. Many sayings in his *Poor Richard's Almanack* are meaningful today; others died or were modified to match new times or places while retaining the basic idea in more modern terms. One such basic idea can serve as an example.

Franklin wrote: *He who hesitates is lost.* Over the years, mothers with daughters changed that to: *She who hesistates is lost.* And today's rush hour drivers prefer: *He who hesitates is rear-ended.*

But a century ago, when that idea came West by Conestoga wagon, Concord stage, or on the rump of a mule, it took on a flavor all its own . . .

The man who straddles a fence
gets a sore crotch.

In Territorial days, young men following Horace Greeley's advice sunk their spurs in the West and didn't put hobbles on the language.

Eeehaw!

So what if great philosophers proclaimed: *A wise man knows his own ignorance; a fool thinks he knows everything.* Those young men changed that thought to this: *Every jackass thinks he's got horse sense.*

Who cared if folks in The Old States were fond of saying: *One man's meat is another's poison.* Cowpokes made the point more colorfully: *A cowchip is paradise for a fly.*

The Auld Sod was a proper place for this old Irish advice: *There are few wild beasts more to be dreaded than a talking man with nothing to say.* But around the corral, this version was it: *The bigger the mouth, the better it looks shut.*

Ain't it a shame we let those Sayin's die just because freeways by-passed the corral? They're as useful today as in Territorial times. And a lot more interesting than pap on the tongue − in the current, not archaic, meaning of the word.

This, then, is what *Savvy Sayin's* is made of: Lean and meaty chunks of Western horse sense with a no-nonsense, colorful candor to match the men and the country.

Where the Sayin's came from

The Sayin's in this book are from the author's collection of old-time Western lore and art. The collection was started in 1950 after listening to old-timer survivors of the Territorial days while on assignments as a Farm and Ranch editor for Arizona newspapers or for magazines covering seven Western states.

Those earlier generations of Americans are now gone but their spirit lives on in the words they left behind. Colorful words that project the personality of the people who said them. Common sense words rooted in the old-time American principles of independent thinking. Slow-talking words, thoroughly chewed before using. Terse words from people with limited or no formal education but words with a profundity and insight that today's best thinkers would be hard-pressed to meet or exceed. For example:

What modern health scientist or diet expert

could really improve on this old advice? *Too much ain't healthy.* It's a textbook in four words.

Or this 100-year-old Sayin'? *Lonesome creates diseases that friendship cures.* The insight of this observation can help explain the recent medical discovery that puppies and kittens can work wonders with residents of retirement or nursing homes.

I was thinking of those Sayin's in July of 1985 while listening to the radio and browsing through my collection of Western lore. Suddenly, the music was interrupted for a bulletin on President Reagan's progress following his operation — reporting with amazement that he was what Westerners would call, "chompin' at the bit to get back to the ranch." Appropriately, a Savvy Sayin' I had been reading jumped off the page: *A year of nursin' don't equal a day of sweetheart.*

If ever there was a person to whom this Sayin' applied — first, following the assassination try and then, his operation — it certainly was the President. He obviously prefers the sweetheart kind of nursin'.

I marked the Sayin' and sent it to Nancy Reagan with the suggestion she show it to the President's doctors. She replied, *"I do think more doctors should realize (that this could be) the Real Reason for speedy recoveries . . . more people could probably go home much sooner!"*

The letter left me wondering whether other old Sayin's could have modern application — one such as this favorite of mine: *Stay shy of a man who's all gurgle 'n no guts.*

Now there's advice with real meat to it. Who do you think might say something like that? In these days of slick-tongued spokesmen and packagers of political images, there's only one public person I can think of whose on-the-record statements could match the no-nonsense clarity of that line — Barry Goldwater, former Senator from Arizona.

I sent the Sayin' and a few dozen more selected examples to him saying I was thinking of putting my collection into book form. He replied, *I think you have one heck of an idea. All of us who were born out here have forgotten the way our fathers and grandfathers spoke, and if we had remembered it, we would all be a lot better off. The Lord knows you understood them when they got it done. Thanks for doing this.*

This was getting to be fun.

I hunted down another colorfully-pungent Savvy Sayin' and sent it off to Henry Kissinger, famed in past administrations for his Shuttle Diplomacy. Would he appreciate the subtle diplomacy of this old Sayin'? *Treat mule-headed men the same way you'd treat a mule you're fixin' to corral. Don't try to drive 'em in. Jus' leave the gate open a crack 'n let 'em bust in.*

We'll never know what Dr. K. thought. He didn't answer. Perhaps in diplomatic circles there are no mule-headed men — just statesmen with firm convictions.

While these letters were fun, they also were beginning to sprout a germ of an idea. Some of the old Cowboy Sayin's sounded vaguely familiar — not because of the actual words used, but in the basic thoughts they expressed. Could they be examples of what happened when The King's English was translated into Cowboy Lingo? Some research was called for.

I started thumbing through the books of proverbs and maxims on my shelves. And soon I hit pay dirt in one of my old favorites — one published in London in 1733, back when they still used the funny-looking "s" which was shaped like an "f" and still capitalized words in the middle of a sentence. The quaint, tongue-boggling title of the book is *Gnomologia: Adagies and Proverbs. Wife and Witty Sayings. Ancient and Modern. Foreign and British.* Certainly anything found in this old book would predate any Cowboy's Savvy Sayin'.

Here's one Olde English example and its Savvy Sayin' counterpart. O.E.: *The Sussefs of*

Malfactors, authorizes not the crime. The Savvy Sayin' counterpart: *A rustler who's never been chased by a posse thinks it's his right to steal*.

Could this old Sayin' have been coined by a British settler carrying back-home ideas to the new land? An interesting theory. What I needed was to find a real expert in The King's English. But where?

The answer came on the 10:00 news — a shot of Prince Charles and Lady Di taking their son to his first day of school. Charles fit the bill perfectly. He was undeniably British. He certainly knew The King's English. He was wild about Cowboys and the West as a youth. He had a well-known love of horses and riding. And unlike other, urban (and urbane) riders, he was unafraid of getting on a horse capable of throwing him once in a while. In fact, if you had followed the gleeful reports in the press of his every spill, you could easily get the idea that he had been thrown often enough to qualify for the ProRodeo circuit.

So I gathered up about 20 old Sayin's having to do with riding. About half of them dealt with getting thrown — Sayin's like: *There ain't a horse that cain't be rode. There ain't a man that cain't be throwed*.

Perfect. But where to send them?

I called the British Embassy saying I wanted

to write to Prince Charles, could they give me his address? And a broadly-accented woman replied, *Well, I should just send it to Buckingham Palace. Someone there is sure to have heard of him.* (And Rodney Dangerfield thinks that *he* "don't get no respect.")

I sent the package, carefully noting on the calendar that it should arrive by Wednesday so I would be sure to stay at home — in case the Prince should phone, you see.

The preceding Monday, there was an account in the paper about some cheeky Britisher who had just written a book poking fun of the Royal Family's accent. He singled out Charles for special mention, saying that the Prince was a defender of the tongue. And, the article added, the Prince spoke as if he had a plum in each cheek. Worse, he titled the book *The Queen's English,* hardly the ideal staging for my letter on The *King's* English due to arrive in two days time. I chalked off the whole idea to a waste of postage.

Six weeks later, a letter arrived from London. This was it!

Well, sort of. It was a letter from Charles' assistant private secretary saying that the Prince had asked him to write. Whereupon, the asst. sec'y. soundly established his credentials for the job. In two short sentences, he managed to say virtually nothing while citing the Prince as saying, *Thank you very much . . . most grateful . . . your kind thought . . . sincere thanks . . . best wishes.* Even when read aloud with a plum in each cheek, there was no meat to support my theory. But he did manage to slip in one interesting word. He said the Prince thought the enclosures (including the 20-odd Sayin's, we presume) were *interesting.* So it was not a total loss.

For those of you who are curious about such things, the stationery was about half thick enough to qualify as a thin, light-weight cardboard, making it difficult to fold without wrinkling. The paper's watermark showed it was made by the *Original Turkey Mill* in Kent. The top was embossed with *Buckingham Palace* and a crown circling three feathers embellished with a banner bearing the motto *Ich Dien,* which in German means *I serve* — a hold-over, apparently, from the days when the official language of this Royal Family was German.

The letter arrived in a plain white envelope with no return address and a beautiful commemorative stamp of David Niven.

So much for scholarly research. Let someone else do it.

But before closing this section, I'd like to share

one more example of the timeless quality of these old-time Sayin's — this involving a person who shall remain nameless.

She was a cute little slip of a woman. Pert, pretty and in her young 30s. All duded up in her Western clothes befitting her job as manager of a posh resort motel in Oak Creek Canyon, Arizona.

I showed her one of the Sayin's: *Never trust a man who kin look a pretty woman in the eye.*

She blinked, pounded her fist on the counter and said, *Ain't that the truth. Them sonsabitches will look you straight in the eye and tell you any thing comes to mind just so's . . .*

I guess those old-time, stove-in cowhands knew what they were talking about. Old truths never die. Some don't even fade away.

A publishing hobby is born

As mentioned earlier, the collection of Sayin's was started while working as a writer around the West. Even when I got tired of being borderline broke and went "Back East" for greener pastures, the collection grew from an increasing number of books, magazines and newspapers published during or about the West of the 1800s.

In 1979, after years of writing jobs around the country, Joann and I retired to Arizona. It lasted six months.

The move had required sorting through the stacks of old books and collections of Western lore and art. And from those stacks and that chore, a new hobby of publishing old West lore was born. It's our retirement alternative to Arts & Crafts, Spanish as a Second Language, and Bring-Your-Own-Water Panning for Gold in a Dry Gulch.

It also is a great way to pay for our summer travel around the West because we load up to half a ton of publications in the station wagon and hit the road, selling out of the wagon as we go. Which has one slight problem — we don't always make it back to the same dealers each year. Plus one not-so-obvious benefit — we get to see lots more places and meet lots more nice people.

Our dealers tend to be concentrated in areas that fit well with our ideas of retirement travel: Near the more spectacular scenic spots, National Parks and Monuments, theme parks and restored ghost towns. Places like Tombstone, San Francisco, Fish Camp, Las Vegas, Cripple Creek, Santa Fe, Grand Canyon and, of course, Denver every year. One of our daughters lives there.

On the way we meet a cross section of people

you rarely read about or see on the 10 o'clock. Wholesome, happy families on vacation from around the world. Mom and Pop retailers pleased as pups about doing their independent thing. Rodeoers and river raftsmen. Surveyors and salesmen. A storefront lawyer from Haight Asbury who is a political conservative. Waitresses with babyfat cheeks and a giggle or sore feet and a smile.

As we ride, we try to outdo each other in spotting unusual businesses: *Paradise Apartments & Used Cars,* in Missouri. *Demolitions & Antiques,* near Durango. *Buck's Free Skunk Removal Service — Now $5,* high up a Rocky Mountain road.

We slow down for deer and armadillo. Wait for a Navajo girl to drive her sheep across the road. Picnic at Grand Canyon with a coyote and Jays waiting for handouts. See the sights while calling on concessionaires at tourist attractions. And try to explore different areas each year.

When we get home, there are the phone calls and letters. Readers who have written or phoned from all the lower 48 states plus Alaska, Canada, England, Sweden, Germany, Holland and Japan . . . people with postmarks not nearly as exciting as The White House or Buckingham Palace or the U.S. Senate, but people with quietly interesting lives.

There's the lady in England who confesses to

a bit of a weight problem from a love of whipped cream with her strawberries. She sends picture postcards of towns where I was stationed before D-Day. The boy in Oregon who sent some Bunkhouse Windies he learned from his pioneer grandfather. A man in Illinois who is *memorizing the old sayings and getting a reputation as the smartest man in the county.* The prospector in Alaska who'd *rather be in Arizona, come winter,* and had his general store stock our items for him and his buddies. The cowhand who needed another copy *'cause m'wife cut up the first one to decoupage the bedroom door with the pictures.* Wonderful folks, every one.

The illustrations

The first illustration in this book is a steel engraving. The rest are woodcuts from the 1800s.

To the uninitiated, woodcuts are made just as the name suggests. The illustrations are cut or carved out of wood. And the carving is done on the end grain of the wood — meaning, if you slice a 2-inch piece out of a tree trunk or branch, the part without the bark is the end grain. It can withstand the hundreds of pounds pressure of a printing press better than the long grain section of wood.

Working from an artist's original drawing or

painting, the engraver would sketch a mirror-imaged copy of it on the wood — mirror-imaged because when the woodcut's ink was tranferred to paper, the image would be reversed back to the original again. Sometimes they goofed. (See Remington's signature in the picture on page 95.)

Then, using engraver's chisels called burins, he would cut out all of the white portions of the sketch, leaving raised areas that made the lines of the illustration — lines which could be inked for printing.

All but two of the woodcuts in this book are the work of America's two all-time favorite Western artists — Frederic Remington and Charles M. Russell. Both knew the West first hand during the peak of the Cowboy era. They traveled the West with the Cowboys and Indians, Generals and Privates, gamblers and miners, prostitutes and bartenders and sod-busters' wives. They saw first hand what made the West work and their work reflected it. The illustrations are from the author's collection.

We hope you will enjoy browsing through these woodcuts and Sayin's as much as we did collecting them and seeing them published again.

Ken Alstad
Tucson

SAVVY
SAYIN'S

Some folks got no more conscience than a cow in a stampede.

A guilty man runs when no one's chasin' him.

The good thing about talkin' to your horse
is he don't talk back.

2

A year of nursin' don't equal a day of sweetheart.

A snake-bit man is afraid of a rope.

Sweat is a waste of whisky.

Kiddin' some folks
is like kickin'
a loaded polecat.

A cowchip is paradise for a fly.

When you scalp a man more'n once, you begin to run out of hide.

Carnation Milk, best in the lan'.
Comes to you in a little red can.
No tits to pull, no hay to pitch.
Jes punch a hole in the sonofabitch.

Frustration is a stump-tailed horse tied short in fly time.

A go-getter is a cowboy who forgot to hobble his horse.

Buckshot means buryin'.

Every jackass thinks he's got horse sense.

Brains in the head saves blisters on the feet.

You kin never trust women, fleas nor tenderfoots.

4

Remington

Silence can be a speech.

The wildest broncos are those you rode someplace else.

Army mules are branded U.S.
meaning UnSafe at either end.

If you fall in a cactus patch, you kin expect to pick stickers.

It's easier to stand the smell of liquor than listen to it.

If your hoss knew how puny you were, he'd stomp you to death.

A man kin easy brag hisself out'n a place to lean on the bar.

Some folks have the hateful taint of being too soon with everybody

There ain't a hoss that cain't be rode.
There ain't a man that cain't be throwed.

The cards ain't been shuffled good 'less you got a good hand.

The bobcat sure was planned good. He's got two holes in his hide right were his eyes go.

Never approach a bull from the front,
a horse from the rear or a fool from any direction.

Lonesome creates diseases
that friendship cures.

A sure cure for a toothache is to tickle a mule's heel.

Too little temptation kin lead to virtue.

Treat mule-headed men the same way you'd treat a mule you're fixin' to corral. Don't try to drive 'em in. Jus' leave the gate open a crack 'n let 'em bust in.

9

There's a little boy
a'sleepin'
in many a grown man
you'd call sensible.

A mail-order marriage is trickier'n braidin' a mule's tail.

Never gamble with a man who knows both sides of the cards.

The best way to hold cattle in the winter
is to do your sleepin' in the summer.

Men and barbed wire have their good points.

A lot of a man's religion is in his wife's name.

Lawyers get you out'n the kind of trouble you'd never get in if there was no lawyers.

A loose horse is always lookin' for new pastures.

Surprise is a near-sighted porcupine fallin' in love with a cactus.

It's hard to put a foot in a shut mouth.

A man don't have thoughts about women till he's 35. A'fore then, all he's got is feelin's.

Admire a big horse. Saddle a small one.

13

A man who ain't got ideas of his own should be mighty careful who he borrows 'em from.

A pat on the back makes some folks' heads swell.

The West is where water has the same value as blood.

A hoss thief takes one trail.
The posse has to choose from ten.

Some fools think they are smart.

Buckshot leaves a mean and oozy corpse.

High-talkin' kin get you leaded.

Every man is afraid of something.

In a public bath, all men are equal — more or less.

Any rider who brags he ain't been throwed
sure ain't forked no bad 'uns.

It's better to say, "Here's where he ran," than,
"Here's where he died."

No man in the wrong kin stand up agin' a fellow
that's in the right 'n keeps a'comin'.

Stay shy of a man who's all gurgle 'n no guts.

An old timer is a man who's had a lot
of interesting experiences — some of them true.

Some men talk 'cause they got somethin' to say. Others talk 'cause they got to say somethin'.

It's the far-off cows
that wear the biggest horns.

There are two sides to any man's argument. His and the wrong one.

Jus' 'cause a man ain't yet had a chance to steal don't mean he's honest.

You kin be wrong.

If you're lookin' at the danger end of a scattergun, pull in your horns.

You're in trouble if your neighbor's cows hang around your calf pen and bawl.

Damn fool mistakes are made by the other guy.

Outlaws and martyrs are greatly improved by death.

Tryin' to get even is a sure sign someone was wrong.

Skill throws more weight than strength.

Kickin' a man when he's down
sometimes is the only way to make him get up.

When a cowboy's too old
to set a bad example,
he hands out good advice.

Any cowboy who says he ain't never been throwed
is a liar.

Wild oats make a mighty poor breakfast.

Second-hand gold is as good as new.

Be thankful for fools. Without them, none of us
would amount to a damn.

A mule is the bastard child of a jackass.

Nerves is just a case of which end of a six-gun you
happen to be lookin' at.

Jes' 'cause a trapper is a mite whiffy don't mean he'

'fraid of water. Some times he uses it as a chaser.

If your cows tend to have more'n one calf at a time, it could be a disease — one that's fatal for you.

When you got nothin' to lose, try anythin'.

Easy money is like a shadow. The harder you chase it, the faster it moves.

It's harder to make a banker out of a hoss thief than a hoss thief out of a banker.

Some folks ain't got the brains to be hoss thieves.

Caution should not be too cautious.

A man who was born to drown will drown on a desert.

Nobody but cattle know why they stampede
and they ain't talkin'.

An over-polite man is hidin' some mighty unpolite ideas.

It's the switchin' tails that catch the cockleburs.

A cowboy buckin' gamblers don't ride home with his tail up.

Sleepin' late keeps a fellow huntin' his hosses.

You kin cut your throat with a sharp tongue.

A corkscrew never pulled no one out of a hole.

Some folks throw too much dust.

Life is one man gettin' hugged for sneakin' a kiss 'n another gettin' slapped.

A windy is a fellow huntin' grizzlies in camp.

Hoss thieves get hung first 'n tried later.

Sometimes you'll find a heap of thread on a mighty small spool.

Make good or make tracks.

A cow outfit
is no better than its horses.

Hot words lead to cold slabs.

The saloon keeper loves a drunk, but not as a son-in-law.

The higher you climb, the more rocks you have to dodge.

You cain't measure water with a sieve.

Life is like checkers. When you reach the top, you can move wherever you want.

The West is famous for rare and wonderful sights.
But the rarest of all is clean socks in a bunkhouse.

No one wants to steal your troubles. No one can
steal your good deeds.

Lonesome makes friends
of strangers.

Love your enemies
but keep your gun oiled.

Man's the only animal who kin get skun more'n
once.

Do not tamper with the natural ignorance of a
greenhorn.

The best seasoning for range cooking
is a salty sense of humor.

It's a sorry cowhand that'll ride a sore-backed hoss.

The man who apologizes when there ain't no need
knows something you don't.

Never trust a man who kin look a pretty woman in
the eye.

Some men are so well-tempered they can lose it every day and never run out.

If a man who knows you calls you "Mister," he don't think too much of you.

Secrets are easy to hear and hard to keep.

Some cowboys got too much tumbleweed in their blood to settle down.

It ain't against the law to be comfortable.

Shallow rivers and shallow minds freeze first.

Don't repent. Stop sinning.

Only a fool
spends his life
makin' the town smoky.

Hoss thieves should be treated like a treasure —
buried with care and affection.

A takin' man hates to give.

If someone outdraws you, smile and walk away.
There's plenty of time to look tough
when you're out of sight.

A good friend is one who tells you your faults
in private.

Before you go into a canyon, know how you'll get out.

Many things are possible
if you cinch your attention to them.

Play your hand close to your belly.

You can educate a fool but you can't make him think.

Some men are so stingy, they'd skin a flea for the hide and tallow.

It's safer to have a good enemy than a bad friend.

Once you start ridin' the high lines, you can't quit no more'n a loser in a poker game.

It's your own fault if you make friends with a hard case.

A man that draws fightin' wages spends a heap of time lookin' for someone to smoke up.

A hoss that's fed too much
gets ornery.

It's easier to catch a horse than break him.

The ignorant hold up trains 'n stages.
The intelligent steal 'em.

Teeth and memory weaken with age.

You can't be hurt by the words you don't say.

Some folks are so soured on life they can't get the
acid out'n their systems.

The three most fatal diseases in the West are:
Small pox, cholera, and the ignorance to argue
with a long-haired, whisky-drinkin' liar.

A man who tells you he's no fool
has his suspicions.

Never tire a grass horse.

43

Some towns are so small that when
the train pulls into the station, it's out of town.

Some men don't amount to much except around
weaklings.

It's better to get it in the neck after a good time
then a poor one.

Sign in a ranch kitchen:
> *If you're hungry, grab a plate,*
> *You have my best wishes.*
> *But before you pull freight,*
> *Be sure to wash the dishes.*

When a hen cackles, she's either layin' or lyin'.

Most women are as pretty as they kin be.

Hotels in the Territory have hot and cold water. Hot in the summer and cold in the winter.

Small tricks lead to big bullets.

Tin plates last longer
'cause they're easy
to straighten out
after a boisterous meal.

A temper is a valuable thing.
Spend it but don't lose it.

Never trust a man who agrees with you. He's probably wrong.

Pass on good advice. That's all it's good for.

Women have more fun because there's more things forbidden to them.

If you always do right, you will please some folks and make the rest wonder what you're up to.

The pessimist's problem is he thinks the whole world is just like him.

A good drinking buddy never heard the story before.

If a cowboy gets bucked
off a rabbit-shy horse
he gets even.
He makes the horse walk
back to the ranch
all by himself.

Few things are harder to put up with than a good example.

Fear breeds hate.

Eagles don't catch flies.

Married men don't like history too close to home.

Ignorance is expensive.

Sweat never drowned no one.

You can't tell how good a man or a watermelon is till you thump 'em.

A sharp eye
is the mother of good luck.

It's fatal to fumble when pullin' your gun.

Drownin' your sorrows only irrigates 'em.

A rolling roulette wheel gathers a heap of moss.

A man who looks for easy work goes to bed tired.

A thief is like a calf.
Give him enough rope and he'll tangle hisself.

A cat has nine lives but a lie can live forever.

A heavy saddlebag makes a light heart.

A winning poker hand is like a Cowboy's legs:
Few and far between.

When you get up on a mule,
keep your eyes on his ears.

Fear the man who's feared of you.

The man who likes to dabble in gore soon has his appetite for lead soaked up.

A fool kin ask more questions in an hour than 10 savvy men kin answer in a year.

What you cain't duck, welcome.

The fellow who goes around well heeled, sooner or later turns up his toes.

Do not feed nuts to a man with no teeth.

If you want to stay single, look for a perfect woman.

Don't complain of getting old. The only alternative is worse.

The West is a great playground
for young men.

You need spurs on a borrowed horse.

If you wake up feelin' half way 'tween
"Oh, Lord," and "My God," you've overdid it.

Suspicion ain't proof.

For some men, it was too late to get wise the day
they was born.

Some men never marry 'cause the girls' mothers
do not trust them too far 'n the fathers don't trust
them too near.

Marry a woman with brains enough for two and
you'll come out even.

You don't need help fallin' down
but a hand up sure is welcome.

Takin' another man's life
don't make no soft pillow at night.

Shorty didn't know whether to feed or starve his cold so he drowned it.

It ain't no time to enjoy a smoke when you're a'sittin' on an open keg of powder.

What's cheap is expensive.

A man don't get thirsty
till he can't get water.

The biggest hosses ain't always the best travellers.

Even a friendly snake
is an unwelcomed guest.

Age makes a man gentle.

Play 'em high 'n sleep in the streets.

A man kin learn a heap of things if he keeps his
ears washed.

There's no more pleasure in some folks' company than in a wet dog's.

Old age makes you a stranger in your own country.

The man who wears his holster tied down don't do much talkin' with his mouth.

Saddle your horse
before sassin' the boss.

The teepee ain't been built

that'll hold two families peaceably.

A good cowman has to know how to lie
to the tax collector 'n cattle buyers.

Nothin' gets nothin'.

Some folks can't see no higher than the steam from
their own pot of stew.

The wilder the colt, the better the horse.

Advice is handy only before trouble comes.

Some men wouldn't know a cactus if they sat on one.

There's nothin' like layin' on your belly
'n stickin' your muzzle in a clean, runnin' stream.

You've got to
control yourself
before you kin
control your horse.

69

A rustler who's never been chased by a posse
thinks it's his right to steal.

The biggest hole in the money pocket is the one at the top.

It takes six cups of town coffee to equal one of horseshoe coffee.

Little sins are little sins until a big man commits 'em.

Some men think the sun comes up just to hear them crow.

Very few gunmen are hanged by a legal hangman.

'Fore a stable kin get clean, someone has to get dirty.

The man who's always lookin' for trouble hopes he won't find it.

When a woman starts draggin' a loop.
there's always some man willin' to step in.

Some men
are bad
— behind
a bush.

A blind horse
kin see just as well from either end.

When the wolf starts a'roostin' at some other fellow's door, it sure shrinks his howl.

Never straddle a fence. Build one or tear it down.

Calico fever can be fatal for a man's bachelorhood.

There's always someone ready to scratch an itchy trigger finger.

When you see a man sharpenin' the ears of cows, you kin bet he stole 'em.

When you ain't on speakin' terms with the law, it pays to travel light.

If you ain't got a choice, be brave.

Set your pace
by your distance.

A wise cowhand
will have something 'sides a slicker for a rainy day.

Happiness depends more on how life strikes you than on what happens.

If you don't buy what you only want, you'll have money to buy what you really need.

A string around the finger helps you remember. A rope around your neck helps you forget.

It's the man who knows how to die standin' up that keeps a'comin'.

Experience is another word for mistakes.

When thieves are around, money is easier to protect than horses. But a fellow with both cain't be too keerful.

A lot of folks would do more prayin' if they could find a soft spot for their knees.

A politician don't steal elections. He pays for 'em.

A good horse
is never a bad color.

The bad wheel
creaks the most.

A fickle woman and a good-shootin' man are apt to hurt someone.

Sign on a wagon:
> Pickin' up bones to keep from starvin'.
> Pickin' up chips to keep from freezin'.
> Pickin' up courage to keep from leavin'.
> Way out West in No-Man's land.

A pat on the back don't cure saddle galls.

If it ain't broke, don't fix it.

If you have a hill to climb,
waitin' won't make it smaller.

All some hard cases need

is to be scared good 'n hard 'n they'll go back to virtuous.

Range cooks are stove-in cowboys
too gimpy to work cattle.

Laugh when you borrow and you'll cry when you pay.

If you have to prove you're right, you're probably wrong.

A drunken tongue tells what's on a sober mind.

What a patent medicine man tells you, he don't mean. What he means, he don't say.

It don't take long for a gamblin' cowboy to put money in circulation.

Nobody ever died too lazy to take a last breath.

Don't pack hardware for bluff or balance.

Don't count the teeth in someone else's mouth.

Backin' up hard words with gunplay is dangerous business unless you're a top hand at it.

The only place some folks make a name for themselves is on a tombstone.

When there's heroin' to be done,
someone has to hold the horses.

Borrowin' is like scratchin'. It only feels good for a little while.

Age gentles men and whisky.

A bronc rider should be
light in the head and heavy in the seat.

There's no room at the chuck wagon for a quitter's blankets.

Wanderin' around like a pony with the bridle off don't get you to the end of the trail.

Some folks change their minds
as easy as an Injun changes camp.

A high-talkin' man kin quick brag hisself
into buryin' or buzzard bait.

Broke is what happens when you let your yearnin's
get ahead of your earnin's.

Some men get callouses from pattin' themselves
on the back.

If the wife of a patent medicine man kisses you, count your teeth.

You can't get to the end of a trail by wanderin' like a pony who's slipped his bridle.

If you follow a new track,
there ain't no way of knowin'
if the man that made it
knew where he was goin'.

FREDERIC REMINGTON

When a territory gets full of family men

and empty of game, it's time to move on or get married.

Never spur a horse when he's swimmin'.

When two play, one wins.

There ain't no way to practice gettin' hung.

It's less painful to be dead drunk than dead hungry.

If you think you've forgotten something, you have.

A man's eyes tell you what his mouth is a'feared to say.

Some folks are pleased to have a feather in their cap.
Others want the whole war bonnet.

91

Don't trust a wolf for dead till he's been skun.

Out West, every prairie dog hole is a gold mine, every hill is a mountain, every creek is a river, and every prospector is a liar.

When a hypochondriac has measles, he tells you how many.

You kin never trust women when courtin' 'em. They might believe you.

Murderers and horse thieves are often found in a state of suspense.

A prospector is a cowboy with his brains knocked out.

A six-gun might cripple you
but buckshot means buryin'.

Never draw a gun
unless you mean to shoot.

The food on some ranches might be a mite weak-tastin', but the coffee's strong enough to bring up the average.

Don't build the gate till you've built the corral.

You can't beat experience for sweatin' the fat off'n the brain.

The man who can't take a word of criticism hears it the most.

A man who confesses to small faults
hopes you will think he has no big ones.

With the Homestead law, the U.S. is betting you 140 acres that you can't live on it.

It's mighty hard to do what your neighbors ain't.

Every man has equal liberty to seek his own level.

If the coffee tastes like mud, remember it was ground this morning.

Assets are baby donkeys.

For better or for worse means for good.

Whisky makes a man see double and feel single.

Pullin' a loaded rife, barrel first, out of a wagon is like ridin' a mule's tail. Both kin get you gut shot.

Take care of yourself as well as you do your horse and you'll both be healthy.

Lightning does the work; thunder takes the credit.

Range horses are dangerous at both ends.

If someone would pump some water into it, an arroyo would be a river.

A smile from a good woman is worth more'n
a dozen handed out by a bartender.

Skin your own deer.

Never do wrong when people are watchin'.

Drunks sober up. Fools remain fools.

Any cowboy kin carry a tune. The trouble comes when he tries to unload it.

Why is it when it rains good things, we've left our slickers at the wagon?

Two names are too heavy to carry if you're travellin' fast.

Some men got more guts than gumption.

Pullin' up the town to look at its roots
don't help it to grow none.

You don't get splinters
from wrestling
timber wolves.

A heap depends on the breed and age of a dog whether he'll bite the hand that feeds him.

A wink is as good as a nod to a blind mule.

Spread happiness where you go, not when.

You cain't tell how fast a jackrabbit will run by the length of his ears.

Many a thing a man does is judged right or wrong according to the time and the place.

Hanging is a legal death trap.

You kin wash your hands but not your conscience.

Even the biggest ball of twine unravels.

The stuff that makes you tipsy makes you tip your hand.

Secrets are easier heard than kept.

The business end of a six-gun don't pay no interest.

You can't head off a man
who won't quit.

Run when you're wrong.
Shoot when you're right.

You kin talk sense to a smart man but not a fool.

Sometimes it's safer to pull freight
than your gun.

Tryin' to run a brand with a cold iron
don't save no time.

Some folks speak the God's truth only when they
admit to lyin'.

An optimist is a man who, when she says, "I'm
tellin you no for the last time," he says, "I knew
you'd weaken in time."

Some men's wives are angels. The others are still
alive.

Most gunmen
wiggle their
trigger fingers
once too often.

If you toss a rope 5 times and miss,
the only thing left to do is lie.

If she says, "No," you haven't asked the right
question — or the question right.

When things don't please you, the best medicine is
to swallow a little tincture of time.

Priceless ain't free.

Strangers are moreso east of the Missouri.

A stone stops rollin' when it finds the kind of moss it wants to gather.

If you've lived to be 29 and have made no enemies, you're a failure.

When in doubt,
let your horse do the thinkin'.

Tossin' a rope
before buildin' a loop
don't catch the calf.

Important comes in two sizes — yours and mine.

Hate is like water in a dry gulch. The longer it runs,
the deeper it digs.

A wishbone ain't no substitute for a backbone.

112

A good friend is a man
who rolls his own hoop.

113

A cowboy is a hired hand on horseback.

Some folks have their good points but they keep jabbin' you with 'em like they was spurs.

Every town has a couple with the same likes and dislikes: They like to fight and hate each other.

The town drunk has a lot of horse sense. You can lead him to water but he won't drink it.

A confirmed liar is a man who, even when he admits he's lying, no one believes.

It kin be unlucky to postpone a marriage — once.

Never marry a woman with the kind of looks you'd like to see on another man's wife.

The only kind of equality that counts is being equal to the occasion.

Cowboys don't play poker for money. Dealers do.

You can't drive a range-raised horse
over a rattlesnake.

A brave man doesn't admit courage.
Cowards don't admit fear.

116

Many things should be done in silence
and talkin' about them is a mistake.

The rider of a rough string may be short on brains

but not guts.

A man kin die from a good poker hand
— if it's too good, like 5 aces.

Some men never reach a marriageable age.

Arizona is no place for amateurs.

A dead man's shroud has no pockets.

Most folks are just about as happy as they've
made up their minds to be.

Most gossip ain't worth the repeatin' it gets.

A 6-inch rain in Arizona is 1 drop every 6 inches.

Careful is a naked man climbin' a bobwire fence.

Thieves are presumed innocent till proved guilty but a man with a starched collar has to prove himself.

The man who can't make a choice makes a choice.

Men honor men who honor their fellow man.

When you hear night birds call in the daytime
and follow you along the trail,
it's time to head for cover.

It's a sure sign of bad luck
to bet on the wrong horse.

On a gentle horse, every man is a rider.

If you're fixin' to pull freight, do it kind of casual
— like you wasn't even noticin' it yourself.

Some men are like the sky. The only time they're
quiet is when they're blue.

A bronco has to have his spree
when the humor strikes him;
afterwards he'll behave for months.

He thought she was his'n. He learned he was her'n.

You can't tell how far a frog will jump
or a horse will run by the color of his hide.

A loud mouth and a shallow brain go well together.

Hard-boiled eggs tend to be yellow inside.

A self-made man worships his creator.

To avoid temptation, yield.

To learn what money is worth, try to borrow some.

The man who knows the least repeats it the most.

A puny man can't afford to get mad.

Roller towels suffer from
being a mite too popular.

The ranch that has
real milk, butter and eggs
is an oasis in the
Territory's bill of fare.

An Injun haircut calls for
a certain amount of hide.

Foreman: "I'm a man of few words. If I say come,
you come." Cowboy: "I'm a man of few words,
too. If I shake my head, I ain't comin'."

Weigh words, don't count 'em.

Time is the best doctor.

There ain't much paw or bellow
to a man who's sure of himself.

When the law pins a star on a man's brisket,
it don't make him no wiser. But if he don't abuse it,
it gives his wisdom power for right.

Even a blind pig will find an acorn once in a while.

A chip on the shoulder is a sure sign of a blockhead.

If it takes liquor to build your courage, you might
have to prove it.

Always ride on the high side when there's
folks around that ain't declared their intentions.

131

A man is as good as his nerves.

Bein' too positive in your opinions
kin get you invited to a dance — in the street,
to the music of shots, nicely aimed.

Shorty never learned to spell 'cause the teacher kept changin' the words.

Stick your nose in trouble and you're likely to find your foot's in there, too.

Food for thought gives some folks indigestion.

The least said, the sooner mended.

The population of some small towns never changes. Every time a baby is born, someone leaves town.

A man that packs his gun loose don't run his heels over sidesteppin' trouble.

Tex has been crippled up with all the old cattleman's ailments ever since he discovered Red Eye was a good painkiller for all the old cattleman's ailments.

Cowboys are paid $30 a month
to out-think cows.

Don't interfere with nothin' that don't bother you.

It's the little things that get tangled in your spurs that trip you up.

A skunk don't trifle when it comes to his perfume.

A toothless dog chews careful.

136

The farther you run,
the longer the way back.

FREDERIC REMINGTON

By the rules of gunfighting, the loser is wrong.

It takes a range-reared hoss to work cattle
— one that kin rustle 'n live on grass.

Broke is ordering oyster stew 'n hopin' to find a pearl so's you kin pay for the meal.

Some folks look at their own common sense through a magnifying glass.

Don't try to stop a fight till it's over.

A man that's quick of tongue might have to be quick on the trigger.

When a man calls your bluff, it's time to look at your hole card again.

Don't laugh at another hombre's trouble.

Some friends are friends only up to the pockets.

It's the man that's the cowboy
not the outfit he wears.

A tombstone can stand upright
and lie on its face at the same time.

The West don't care what a man calls himself. It's
what he calls others that lets him stay healthy or not.

Life ain't in holdin' a good hand but in playin'
a poor one well.

A politician can borrow $20, pay back $10 and
declare you're even 'cause you both lost $10.

Never try to drown your sorrows if she kin swim.

Approach a mule the way a porcupine makes love:
Slow 'n keerful.

Don't point a gun at nobody
you ain't willin' to shoot, if necessary.

If you want to leave your mark,
don't let the sun catch you in bed.

It's the absent who are judged guilty.

Polishin' your boots on a brass rail is dangerous to
your wealth.

A man who keeps his eyes on the horizon like he's
expectin' the sheriff to budge up on him
has more on his mind than seein' the sights.

A full house divided wins no pot.

A gentle horse is soon curried.

If you'd like to know a man, find out what makes him mad.

A man who hunts trouble in a saloon is apt to pass in his chips with sawdust in his beard.

Many a man would rather leave his hide on a fence than stay in a corral.

You never know your luck till the wheel stops.

You'll never find a hired gun sittin' on his gun hand.

You're bound to succeed if you have ignorance and confidence.

There's always a few longhairs who do their damdest
to fertilize the cow country's reputation for
being wild and woolly.

Some folks follow old wagon tracks.
Others break new trails.

Circuit-ridin' preachers are so poor that if they didn't fast twice a week, they'd starve to death.

You'll sure get out-pointed if you pick a fight with a porcupine.

There ain't many tears shed at a Boot Hill buryin'.

Never pack a 6-gun with 6 pills in the wheel. If you cain't do the job with 5 shots, it's time to get the hell out of there.

Next to hoss rustlin', curiosity is the most dangerous crime.

Anyone kin look tall when surrounded by shorties.

Stealin for charity is stealin'.

Nerve succeeds.

Don't fork a saddle
if you're scared of gettin' throwed.

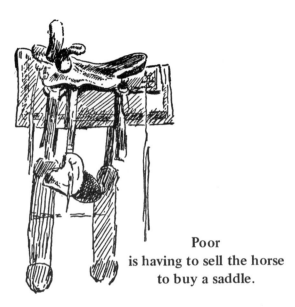

Poor
is having to sell the horse
to buy a saddle.

Do not desire what you can't acquire.

It's easy to fill the shoes of a big-headed man.

The best way to convince a tenderfoot is to let him have his own way.

Ugly women hate mirrors.

A faint heart never filled a flush.

If you see a coward with a gun, it's time to get scared or scarce.

The jealous man soon learns to hate.

The man who keeps a bridle on his temper shoots the truest.

Be mighty careful
in your choice of enemies.

Close friends are folks
who've sopped gravy out'n the same skillet.

Folks that always ride in a high lope miss the fun along the trail.

A change of pasture kin make the calf fatter.

You cain't never tell which way a pickle will squirt.

When the boss wants a long talk, you're in for a long listen.

Don't leave a travelled road to follow a trail.

Young liars turn into old thieves.

**The hottest fire
is made by the wood you chop yourself.**

A man loses his dreams,
his teeth and his follies — in that order.

After some folks tell you all they know, they keep on talkin'.

Worry is like a rockin' horse. It's somethin' to do that don't get you nowhere.

Immigrants coming West to look for gold were born silly and had a relapse.

When you beat a man at his own game,
you've had all the revenge you need
— unless you're a hog.

There's always someone

to take the slack out of a troublemaker's rope.

On a roundup, it's OK to eat with your fingers.
The food is clean.

You cain't hurt a tongue by speakin' softly.

If you must be a fool, be a rich fool 'n people will
treat you like a king.

A crooked tree will never straighten its branches.

It's better to know the country
than to be the best cowboy.

On the range, a man's home is apt to be
his saddle blanket 'n the first thing you know,
he's moved it to Texas.

When wiser men are talkin', let your ears hang
down and listen.

Some folks morals are as loose as a busted egg.

The West is a good country for men and dogs
but mighty hard on women and oxen.

It's all right to take your time in a gun fight
just as long as you're the first to shoot.

Money is like a drunk. The tighter it gets, the
louder it talks.

No matter how hard the winter,
spring always comes.

Adios.